Also by Charles North

Lineups (1972)
Elizabethan & Nova Scotian Music (1974)
Six Buildings (1977)
Leap Year: Poems 1968-1978 (1978)
Gemini (with Tony Towle, 1981)

The Year of the Olive Oil

The Year of the Olive Oil

POEMS BY
CHARLES NORTH

Hanging Loose Press

Some of these poems appeared, in whole or in part, in the following publications: *United Artists, Transfer, Oink!, Columbia, Poetry Project News-letter, Joe Soap's Canoe, The Paris Review, Hanging Loose, Adventures in Poetry, Broadway 2, The Little Magazine, The Poet Exposed, Mudfish, New American Writing, Gandhabba, Aphros,* and *Pequod*; and in the earlier collection *Elizabethan & Nova Scotian Music* (Adventures in Poetry, 1974).

The author is grateful to the National Endowment for the Arts and to the Fund for Poetry for grants which helped support the writing of this book. Hanging Loose Press thanks the Literature Programs of the Endowment and the New York State Council on the Arts for assistance in the publication of this book.

Cover painting by Rackstraw Downes, "Dragon Cement Plant, Rock Crushing Operation (Study)," 1985.

Published by:
Hanging Loose Press
231 Wyckoff Street
Brooklyn, N.Y. 11217

Library of Congress Cataloging-in-Publication Data
North, Charles,
    The year of the olive oil.
    I.Title.
PS3564.069Y4   1989   811'.54   89-15388
ISBN 0-914610-67-8
ISBN 0-914610-66-X (pbk.)

for Paul Violi

Contents

The Year of the Olive Oil

Sunrise With Sea Monster

Well, we either do it or we don't, as the pigeon said to
    the loaf of bread
doubling as the sky, that is, unaffectedly rocky and clay
    gray, the color of rocks
bordering but not reflecting oceans and in particular the
    one that finds its way here
every so often, though not right now; a function of light
    and surface qualities
such as polish, facet, regularity of design,
implied or announced mineral content, the ability to stand
    still in a storm,
and those qualities that enter surface and suffuse it, or
    melt suddenly
into the next door apartment building, swept down into the
    back garden tow,
like transitions whether in writing or in music that aren't
    really transitional
so that cadence is a matter, ordinarily, of being stunned
    rather than construed,
but no diminishment, as in "fancy" and "open fifths" and
    "environmental sweepstakes"

Little Cape Cod Landscape

for Darragh Park

The garbage is bagged, deposited in the dump, and several months later produces its interest, roses.

Late last night some people walking near the harbor were half-bagged and wanted to walk all the way out on the slippery jetty. Their roses were all talk, but they managed to accomplish their goal in spite of their questionable condition. Sleep roses, roses of the derailed train, rose roses and more roses.

The Year Of The Olive Oil

for Yuki Hartman

I sing the olive oil, I who lately sang
The clarinets in their sturdy packing case, the failure
Of the economy to be both seasonal and self-sufficient,
Packed off like cargo ships into the dim asperities of
    twilight.
Spread on Italian bread it became the summer sky—
And sometimes (brittle as failure) as musical as crystal.
One bottle contained all the arts. Another stimulated
    conversation
Which was itself the first pressing.
Darker pressings for the night
And each dawn had its geographical nuances, French and
    Spanish
Greek and Syrian, as on overcast days there were lumps
Of tough, overworked dough, gray and suffocating, with just
    a trace of gloss.
Then success was measured in thinness like an expensive
    watch;
Failures were as muddy as colors mixed by an infant.
Even virtual sewing machine oil, rancid with use, had a
    place
Beside winters when spears of sunlight, like armed tears,
Fenced in flame-blue iris and more ingenious pupil.
There were kingdoms advertising their future connections
(In crystal palaces with silver flags, cork-like minarets)

Fields of long, slender wheat coated with spring rain:
Sharing with the Jams the flow of shade
And with the Glues and Ointments a calculator-like display
Of the forces of temperature and pressure, as on August days
    in city office buildings.
One type was restricted to the human body, as its perfection
    and condiment.
Before this, there would have been no adhesive
For the world scrape, no solution (admittedly fugitive).
Music caught in the throat like peanut butter
And chords were torn apart, something like peaceful
    war-resisters
Until there was little sense of connection.
People read and wrote in fits, misunderstanding the true
    nature of the medium.
Then or soon after the intellect was felt to be
A part of life's suspension, and barbers never had to oil
Their scissors. If there was an occasional
Domestic squabble, it ran to gentle advice.
It is clear that vegetables, as in Andrew Marvell, were the
    chief
Image and model of human desire; and like water off a duck's
    back
— Pressed to golden brown, with pale gold juices intact and
    no fat —
Slid the momentary chagrins and anxieties, the bankruptcies
Spiritual and otherwise — otherwise irremediable; except for
Long slow decanting like passages of pure virgin time.
They had, as far as I can see, no word for friction.

It looked like a partial though real changeover to ball-
    bearings
on the part of even the most adamant faculties of mind and
    body,
Writer's cement block and fractious self-interest group
    (the quiet ferment
Made clear by the necessity to be glass-clad, stoppered)
Enabling human achievement to flourish like a gold breeze,
Circular and reforming in the glow and liquid fragment.

The Postcard Element In Winter

1.

Supposing the wildlife became a person
who suddenly sprouted into an infinite number of ideas
each idea casting an ideal glow from canyon to canyon
like the most wandering star space

whose atmosphere singes the very park—
as though the city existed to be barreled through
in spite of the windy quiet on its face
the factory snap, the raw potatoes and practicing the bassoon

2.

~~Your recent letter is so stupid so utterly moronic its~~
~~a little difficult to believe it was~~
~~written by a human being let alone someone~~
~~who made it past the second grade you~~
~~miserable bastard do you eat~~
~~from a plate~~ thanks for your letter of January 5th
I enjoyed getting it

Two Architectural Poems

1.
Piano and hedges
and more piano,
and sometimes the piano wins.
And sometimes the taxis are movie locations
       set apart from the double
       vision of the city elevatedly
       affixed to see. From storefront
       to riverfront, and from
       middle-income housing mismanagement
       to the unstabilized, stable
       poor. The bits of piano
       coating the hedges, turned
with only an occasional cloud to spill,
to fix the objects that would be there
if it weren't; powder blue and vertical
rather than one limit in a vast evening field.

2.

As the Pleiades hasten to their
unilluminated shore, sanded by new geographies,
so the fluted columns and freshening
ruins (like a sleepless night filled
        with starlike address books)
        outpace their initials
        without sacrificing dawns
        either of rough-cut or blinding
        continuity. Uncurled in figuring,
        the vaguest action, an avenue
        rushes past its name only to govern,
        like a square in London,
the long-lashed, flecked, coastal
and approximately Art Deco sunlit upper storeys.

Prometheus At Fenway

Carl Yastrzemski, the Boston Red Sox outfielder/first baseman, and Prometheus, the carrier of fire and its related arts to humans, are tragic heroes in the Aristotelian sense of the term. Both are champions, both suffer reversals as a result of a mistake or character flaw inextricable from their greatness, and both are ultimately redeemed, though in different ways.

Prometheus the Titan, punished by Zeus for stealing fire from the Olympians and thereby saving humankind, suffers through many lifetimes chained to a rock in the unpleasant Caucasus. Each day a vulture or eagle gnaws at his liver, and each day the liver grows back. Rather than repent or try in any way to placate the god, Prometheus is defiant throughout, thereby adding greatly to his difficulties. Carl Yastrzemski, in the modern Caucasus of baseball, improves his strength at a gymnasium one winter and the next season leads the American League in batting average, home runs (tied) and runs-batted-in. The Red Sox, proverbially good "on paper" and wilting in the strong sun of September, are saved from their reputation and win the American League pennant. At the height of his powers, trying to make the extraordinary usual, Yastrzemski begins to swing for the fences, sees his average, home runs and rbi's fall off dramatically, and the Red Sox go eight years minus a reminder of their flare of glory. His fans silently plead with him to meet the ball, but he continues to swing so hard he nearly falls down.

Prometheus literally (or semi-literally) and Yastrzemski figuratively are chained to their errors-cum-excellence: in Prometheus' case a strong sense of Self tinted by a rather stubborn self-righteousness (mitigated, it must be said, by the encouraging knowledge that he will live to see his tormentor's downfall); in Yastrzemski's case an unreliably expanded Self-image, possibly helped along by an inflated salary. This is before "free" agency. Prometheus eventually emerges free and victorious, a model, among early role-models, for humans. Yastrzemski returns to his real strengths: singles and doubles; skillful running, fielding and throwing, plus a flare for the extraordinary in all three; and a sense of his limits as player, person and hero, helping the Red Sox to their third pennant drive (stalled in the World Series) and ensuring himself via skill and "longevity" of a place in baseball's Hall of Fame in Cooperstown, N.Y.

"Carl" is a form of "Charles," which is a form of "chain." Both Southampton and the Caucasus are difficult to farm (though each produces its own memorials: time- and space-bound myth, potatoes, paintings, the rarer virtues of necessity). Yastrzemski left Notre Dame after his first year, finishing up later at Merrimack; Prometheus never went to college, but showed good insight especially concerning others, the courage of his convictions, and that pranks can be more important than they initially appear. Yastrzemski isn't a big man by sports standards; Prometheus gained and lost every day.

In point of fact, Fenway Park has been a *tragic floor* for better than fifty years, in spite of — and in part because of — those exceptional years 1967, 1975 and 1946, and the well known generosity of the late Irishman Tom Yawkey. The Green Monster is Boston's vulture, each day tearing out the hearts of its passionate fans many of whom live in and around New York and returning them dramatically the next. Batting third in their respective lineups, in the prime of their lives, neither Prometheus nor Yastrzemski can quite locate the "UP" elevator of Fortune. Yastrzemski strikes out by overswinging; Prometheus can't even take a shower. Both were originally from the tip of Long Island but not Southampton proper. Both had a mission from the time the atmosphere was distinctly semi-pro. Both were booed. Yet each developed an exterior that was tough *and* appealing: a gritty appeal: resolution and independence and more than a hint of helpless pig-headedness, tempered by a complete absence of the usual self-interest (as evidenced, among other things, by Yastrzemski's relatively moderate super-star salary, Prometheus' almost callous disregard for his own welfare); or certainly no more than is usual, merging at all points with the larger concerns of the group in a rare display of *knowledge* and *power* so unaffectedly conjoined that Yeats who naturally comes to mind begins to embarrass with his "elevated horniness" and questions designed to take the reader's mind off the real issue ("loosening thighs").

Each expands in time or something like it; Yastrzemski merging with the single-minded, almost too brilliant, driven and child-like whipped brilliance of Ted Williams, and on back to the folly of Babe Ruth; Prometheus undergoing metamorphosis after metamorphosis, expanding and contracting both (in the heroic mode of The Incredible Shrinking Man, whose resonance and

historical aptitude are in direct proportion to his gradual diminish-
ment), beyond the incredible folly of his brother Epimetheus
towards the undiminished atoms of Lucretius and Democritus,
until it is obscure whether there is a universe apart from the chorus
of scintillae that impinge on our competitive painterly conscious-
nesses guaranteeing our apparent freedoms, as against their dark
green, almost black background and still darker energy source,
running the turf of our years.

Tinker To Evers To Randomness

Most of matter is space; and
the spatial is a kind of industrial
solvent always being offered at
a discount, like new shopping malls
            forever unfolding
            newer ones, which stretch
            not the ideal land- or air-rights
            but the modern account (like a series
            of transparent mailboxes each of
            which holds a future at
            least in potential); which is
            not to say that quartz-like
            there are no urban creatures to shine, or
that out of the blue the urban moonlight
fills the canyons as against the
sheer idea of technique, windblown
skidding like our wildest dreams.

Naming Colors

A perfect cream
                    its middle reaches up
Wheaties ravishes the lower two-fifths
Geraniums thin as boxers' ears rip
The hem and catch light stars falling

And hair like a constellation of winter
Vegetables redeems the purple plain
Acorn squash, Idaho potato, philodendron,
Raw chestnut and grape ivy sweep the page

And become the pink and the lighter blue

A Note To Tony Towle (After WS)

One must have breakfasted often on automobile primer
not to sense an occasional darkening in the weather joining
     art and life;
and have read *Paradise Lost* aloud many times in a Yiddish
     accent

not to wake up and feel the morning air as a collaborator
thrown from some bluer and more intelligent planet
where life, despite the future's escalating ambitions, has
     ramified

in every direction except UP; and have been asleep a long
     time
in the air bonded to night not to feel the force of the present
shimmering in the downtown buildings, like European walled
     cities

whose walls have all but disappeared via benign invasion
and touristic drift, even the World Trade Center
for all the enigmas concerning *who* is trading *what* to *whom*,

and while deracination is fast qualifying as essence
rather than attribute, towards the brush with open sea.

April

To normal seeing, a cloud that is also known,
as to the air branches are contrast as well as harmony.
Time is one answer, but space has a will of its own.

Thus when we say anything is *known*
we mean the air supporting it (sometimes violently,
to normal seeing the cloud that is also known)

is moved by what was formerly known
to disclose its presence, even indistinctly.
Time is one answer, space has a will of its own.

If it verges on the separation between known
and knower, the moving back and forth not exactly
spatial and even less in time (normal seeming plus known
    clamor)

then seeing takes place regardless of what is or isn't known —
seeing air like this, on the verge of entity
time being one answer, space having a will of its own.

Which will flowering as though on its own
(while the sun burns and powders over the burned-in city)
is normal seeing, a cloud that is also known
if time is one answer, if space has a will of its own.

A Note On Labor Day

for Paula

Sometimes I think I'm
close to discovering
why half my life has occurred
in a fog, which makes
the other half radiant
by comparison.
The wind,
September's ship,
blows some pigeons
out of a blue and white voiceless fog
off the cornice. Another
flock, atmospherically vague,
is flowing east: a rather pale gleam
with fragments of a greenish metal
embedded in it, among
them a starfish complete
with notes on its history.
Musical ones.
And I seem to be
lost again, if that doesn't
sound too dramatic,
and this time seems worse,
or around the slightly silvered bend
slightly blurred in late sun
that has some whirling filters over it

mostly for the jackets and books.
The cars
stay close to the ground
to be near the trucks.
The busses and taxis move heaven
and earth to be near anyone.
And a green chair floats heavily
to earth smelling like burning leaves,
crushing some Americans
who were unwilling to work.
Armless, legless and backless
chairs—ah your back, that field.
If picture-taking
is discussed at all
and it isn't, the notes
go up in smoke—from
a wood fire, thick and concealing nothing.
The sky gets off its cot;
shoves some pamphlets into the giant blue hand
(the way Nixon pushed Ziegler)
holding the drink,
as mindless as mindless city planning.
A school of fish pass in the bright sunlight,
a bike is stolen and lofted
into the chilly air over Riverside Park,
sentenced to be held without trial
each afternoon succumbing
to the green of each evening
with no hope of putting it off.

Sirens whoop and swallow the earth.
Indigestible!
And flat!
To lie along its surface, walk
around as we all do
even the Flatiron Building—
in the middle of the general
unresolve that untangles
itself once a day to hang
just outside the window sill,
somewhat humiliated,
like dusk, and caring
only in wildly scattered notes.
So a tugboat has plowed
up Broadway pulling half
the Battery behind it
and a moving van roars by, throwing
minor problems into far-flung relief
except for a barking dog which heaves
a luminous sigh. . .too explosive
still, for the pigeons,
but thick enough
to cover the peeling paint
and traffic passing, passing
under cover of dusk
which was the underpainting of its wish.
The pen being an extension
of the arm, coffee rushes
into it, saved from dislocation

by some purple flames at the top: accompanied
by a kind of fugue starting
in the sewers—alligator youth band
plus a few bright rats to fill
out the strings, ah music—
as a testimonial
mostly confused
to Brahms sentinel and chief persuader
(vice-president Jean Siméon Chardin,
secretary Andrea Palladio) as that
snowy city piles on others and
the process rapidly reverses, like
the Falls at St. John's,
which are to this bright late day as blue
to peaked snow. Of the twelve
ways to success, one
is not taking the window
off its sash and throwing
it down onto the street, where
it crashes like a tennis racket
onto the head of an Australian
who took a wrong turn.
Like an awkward, but
awkwardly staying dream;
that the dream is always in
Spanish, always held over,
throwing the air across the way
into mental confusion like a surprise
quiz, on the entire planet

of reference, with terracing
on all sides to provide a quick aisle,
visually, to accidents,
bank robberies, lovers' quarrels (stabbing
at the corner leaving about
fifty yards of blood)
and holiday quiet, withdrawn
and hardly able to speak
though not from not wanting to,
the way the roof separates
exaggeratedly revealing the moon,
with yellow hair, worn
close and tied at the
back into a kind of ponytail,
with a tortoise-shell barrette, to
make you easier to find.
And a subway stumbles
clatteringly on into the night
carrying the hopes and fears of absolutely no one.
Instead, a suspended life burying
its head in the paper, or paper bag,
together with a cockroach
the size of a small dog, who
comes forward occasionally
to sample the cooking and the clothes
or carves a road on someone's
stranded wakefulness, to confuse matters
further. Now the coffee is gone,
like the pigeons, back

into the cannon until
some backfire or genuine shooting
sends them crashing off
the roof in an avalanche of
domestic tranquility scattered
to the four winds —
with lips that part sometimes
to stagger the imagination, like
Aphrodite's breasts. Ships,
brilliant apartment buildings facing west
all the purposes and prospects
none of which are mine, how can
I be so frantic as I sometimes
seem, or do I want to be
thought so, and by whom.
And by whom not, talking
not to talk, to distract
the orders who have our mouths and lingual structure
— or yours, you critical schmuck.
Trees wave on the roof
across the street
which has the forsythia for two weeks
every year, which I always want you
to paint, which is past,
or almost, as light sweeps it
diagonally across the frontier
between reality and metaphysics, with some
early fall smells for a walking stick.
Metaphysics takes

strong exception — fortunately
it speaks only German, and stutters.
If someone is hammering
below, smoothing out our street,
no one is fixing coffee in
a room gradually filling with paintings,
each transforming the room into
an awareness of its lack,
or mine, leaving music
as the prime consolation for the inability
to leave the body, except insofar
as music throws off her clothes
to reveal her secret self:
the absence of a secret.
Such a metallic light on that roof — like
braces on a rabbit.
People crawl to work,
crawl to lunch, crawl to coffee break,
crawl to the subway, and the bin
and home, its obscured
vision lately like a meadow
overwhelmed by goldenrod, among the more
disturbing and radiant overtones, and a
newspaper weighted with cement
cracks against the garage door
and stars are catapulted across
the lawn to catch on the telephone wires: banded
with lindens in a reverse twist
as if the air were

a part of the earth, and waking
required only a slight elevation.
Every twenty minutes.
Which means getting up
from the couch (spinning)
and seeing the sky radically changed
from its previous appearance
— like a gull that dropped
through the 7 stages of life
in a single afternoon —
as a giant clam pushed slowly
over Riverside Park, in mild hopes
of dinner under the stars,
its muscles gradually faltering
though not without a certain
pleasure in being eaten by
discriminating people who chose
this time and place to appear in.
Or not to disappear from.
The ocean is mainly a difference
in scale — sun streaking
boards in preference to sky
whose spangling is threatening to take
over the earth — allowing for
vacation time, thunder heads,
insect bites, the pull of
work and the rest. Sleep
douses it like so much dust to be swept.
Meanwhile the building, shaded

lighter towards the top,
has been picked up and deposited
in another warp, suffering
mainly from reference shock,
with only the books and
records intact, as predicted
by several of them.
The light changes state.
Changes again.
The animals have done
only half the work which has
to be completed by nightfall
and the teams are warming up.
A weasel (?) just emerged from the clubhouse
carrying a woman. Critics chase both away.
Traveling at the speed of light
to be elsewhere, in the dream
which is the subject of Spanish poetry
or the *which*, which seems French...
your hair lagging behind your cheek
the pupil is flushed and held
accountable for the darker haze
of its surroundings, which is night
taking my breath away.

Looking At The Brighter Night

You get to feel the limits of framing, not unlike
Charles the Bad (d.1387) who having been sewn into
a sheet soaked with brandy by doctors who thought
alcohol a panacea, and who then held up a lit candle. . .
the idea being that the form proclaims
the *formless*, regardless of night and its celebrated reductions
linking all things to their proper names,
Bar des Bouqinistes et Filles aux Cheveux de Lin,
Cheap Passage to Natchez, Harborside Cock
and Pullet (England); O city tromboned beyond its poles

View From A High Ledge

My spiritual idiocies for
want of a better word
aren't entirely spiritual, but they
do edge over towards something
       a good ways from matter
       while occasionally plowing into it.
       On target in other words
       despite rough waters, like
       hitting a barn door on the head.
       The rocks being clearly
       in sight, it isn't so much
       a matter of the dark beaming forth,
good tidings spread like a net over the sea,
but its silent and mostly arbitrary correction;
as the trees are arbiters of all you intercept,
the islands bodies drinking in the waves.

For A Cowper Paperweight

Not that his writing isn't moving when
it doesn't seem it should be,
owing in part, at least, to the cloud of difficulty
surrounding his difficult life,
the pleasure of the low key
and mastery of cadence—but that it is
difficult to say why some of it
should be as good as it is, the life
of the writing apart from the life.
The quiet assertions made,
assertion becomes an extended lyric
which, foregoing rapture (as it foregoes
rhapsody) presents feeling in such
a way that it ascends human heights,
both detailing and depending on
the level motion of the feeling tone,
like a long headline broken up into
individual letters and presented
at random, one letter at a time
throughout long and occasionally tedious
narrative and description, the promise of sunshine
throughout a long brightly overcast afternoon.
(As though—almost—one had to compete
with the weather and lose in order
to feel anything, or as though mere utterance
blended one with what was being uttered,

in this case ground and sky, the nature
and numerous pleasures of being between.)
Nor do the exceptions in what prevails,
"I was a stricken deer, that left the herd
Long since; with many an arrow deep infixt
My panting side was charg'd," alter
the weather of the context, while lending a sense
of extra, unrepressed life to the whole;
to a whole consisting of dullness
as well as all the other neighboring kingdoms.
A sense that pleasure is often
pleasure of recognition which doesn't depend
on prior experience — though one has had that too.
"Oh Winter, ruler of th'inverted year,
Thy scatter'd hair with sleet like ashes fill'd,
Thy breath congeal'd upon thy lips, thy cheeks
Fring'd with a beard made white with other snows
Than those of age, thy forehead wrapt in clouds,
A leafless branch thy sceptre, and thy throne
A sliding car, indebted to no wheels,
But urg'd by storms along its slipp'ry way,
I love thee, all unlovely as thou seem'st,
And dreaded as thou art!"'

Poem For Trevor Winkfield

Two mops are cavorting in the next world.
"What do you do?"
"Nothing! I don't do anything!"
Orange light, then darkness. Then orange light.

Sonnet

The dream: to have
more time.
And suppose you could have all the time?
Someone walks up and deposits
in your outstretched hand,
not time exactly; but
of all that is circumambient,
all that pure aura, the infinite possibility
that although no one thing is lost
nothing is exceptional.
Leaves pry out the distance
between new construction and the old
bright lights, massed for waterfront
and mixed use alike. The painter
pulls back, shades his eyes.

Criticisms Of Montauk

The wash is shepherded from one tree
or flattened human signpost to another
less *philosophical* than concerned for philosophy
brained by sunlight making all talk an aside
— as though we just float like the White House on a $20 bill

      — it's interesting how, apart from tracking
      light takes on an outline of its own
      as it were envisioning itself like a lobster in a sunset
      the care all-too-human logic takes for all-too-human
          beauty
      which pulls the mallows from their prospective beds

Nocturnes

1.

Suppose the impossible: that the *peeing* were the romantic part, and the *screwing* made everybody leave the room. Except you of course, and the night and its meteoric music. Persons skate by like un-delivered (and undeliverable) groceries, freaked by discourse, as if that were a function of the charge: to board up windows in a skyscraper and have someone or some thing break through peri-odically. But the gods are drunk; and the large suitcases lining up until some threaten to be architecture, or at worst architectural sculpture, are inclining towards New Jersey; some semi-glittering en route.

2.

While the Romantic contribution — that one sees oneself by per-
ceiving landscape, since projection is the yew tree of life — thins
out into the wash of latter-day psychoanalysis, so ornament dur-
ing the time the light actively settles means what it says it means.
The half-buildings in the narrow world have fallen asleep. A yellow
light is emanating from the brain over the Hudson River. If you
took up the visible threads and glued them, so they formed one
dark gray thread with highlights that implied and also severed all
connections, then the present roof together with its one-time cornice
would enact the precise texture it needs from the virtual — it looks
like a horizon — fragment above, outlasting along a different
perspective line as the narrow world outlasts its own formations,
the state of grace being fed by nothing so much as sheer presence.

3.

The gods are fighting to stay awake. Just now one hurled some-
thing over the drawn-in end of the river below. Everything is
subsumed, the sleep of landscape, the flowers in the window box
existing when no one is looking, the street with its bone china and
animadversions towards roots of daylight. Time stops gamely. A
large bloodshot eye encircled by small gray cumulus clouds behind
a white shade, a smudge near Mercury, twin towers at the far end
of the spectrum, an inverted pyramid of cheese, tomatoes, and extra
cheese. Moments hurtle through over and below open and closed
windows scattering crystals, roars of houseplants. The far piling
marbled with green and white light, transfixing the Northeast, is
Discord.

4.

I'm thinking of a state somewhere between the existing one and its existing surface, soaked with all that upholds. Angels wearing coats of bread crumbs and orange peel, all the talk about subject being a kind of fanfare rather than returning to the sign, which signifies a rather dark night for poetry despite its ailerons, colored blue as the moon. There is a small explosion of time, as well as additional space to hold it; yet all the space is filled. Yet there is still space as, strictly speaking, you can't emerge from time dripping with anything let alone a significant life riveted to its after-effects; the linear red implying all that can be said without coming right out and inhabiting a different language; the broken lines and borders intervening on the tree side; the people and their outlines, out of focus and then sharp indeed.

5.

One table is philosophical, two are Hegelian, and three the main
reading room in the library, and if the darkness is *expected* then it
isn't darkness. Which is a start; especially considering the drops
of floodlight pushed into place, one bear or raccoon picking his
way into the oncoming traffic which is legion. The outline grows.
Philosophers say you can be shipwrecked from too much thought.
They say walking on two feet mars the soul, which is tied to the
earth in bunches like glass rods gathered into millefiori, glowing
pebbles piling up. But the piling could well be the "other" which
would help explain its appeal to outer space; and the ocean or in
this case the bay ("I am not now, nor have I ever been, a creative
writer") clams up as usual.

6.

Just as there is no legitimate beginning the Broadway buildings burst into light. Clothing stores, judicial quarters, restaurants riveted by the full extent of the law, hammering perquisites such as the scored half of the sky, hitting spoons and much too polished foreheads. Like thick, thick hair that has just been washed and is staying in place. Or dry, is combed and, fuller, grows more reflecting of its immediate surroundings in which other heads are being washed, being equal in value and texture to the undivided moment. The auxiliary scoreboard just lit up.—Has there been a takeover or leveraged buyout of the dark elements by the far less numerous bright and immediate, amounting to a virtual solar system racing within the confines of our orbit?

7.

I'm not dismissing it. My heart goes out to those who write, "You really helped with my writting." The pigeons inside the window touch the sky. Or would, if the sky would look down for once without worrying about who is painting it and how long the influence will last, and whether each new substrate removes a portion of history from the readily apparent, the barrels of humidity being launched over the falls that, for most of us, define our becoming lighter even than our mental events. So much *air*, so much sky — and levita-tion — so many surfaces splintered, newly scored, pried away to form families of surfaces, something like the flattened communities layering southern Florida. Whereupon the cars become trucks and are carrying, with a great deal of noise and effort, the north-south cordage without stopping, even for lights.

Late Prelude

Or original stars, plus the altruism
of not knowing what to play. . .

while the taxis resolve
to vanish from the face of the earth

to the face behind it, wrapped in
the dreamlife like a piece of fried fish.

It's difficult to get the news
from the newspaper, yet someone sliced a cabbage

which keeps circling, slice by opaquer slice
over the river and its gaudy landfill

—further; like a new Woolworth Building
the same except that it is not as it was before it changed

Clarinet

after André Chénier

Less than a recurrent dream, but more haunting.
The clarinet is poised and I begin playing,
conscious of occupying some exact center
where I am both rival and conqueror.
My usually awkward embouchure
produces tones which are inspired and pure.
Its fingers latch on to mine and hold on tight,
lifting and dropping them until *I* get it right,
over and over. As though beauty entered will,
brightening and darkening the resonant bell.

On The Road

after Colin Muset

And when I see winter coming on
I feel like staying put.
If I could find the right host
who had more than enough and didn't care,
books, records, a comfortable house in the country,
a lot of bread, a lot of cheese, and a lot of beer,
the kids happy, baseball just in case
and you beside me in the wilderness. . .
and if his wife is as generous as he is
and always thinks of my pleasure first,
days and nights for as long as I've been here
(with no hint of jealousy on his part,
no choosing not to leave us entirely alone)
then I would forget all about this writing business,
all the bad stretches and muddy turnings-off,
plus a lot of general unpleasantness besides.

Fourteen Poems

Similarly; whereby the current polarization
Holds out little hope for lasting revision

*

Meanwhile tragedy outgrows its religious
Origins in an effort to encompass

*

A dip in air pressure, the sense that daylight
Has slipped from its porch onto the grassy night

*

Need, ambition, unrest, and one-dimensional
Thinking latticed on a horizon of metaphysical

*

Rather than its extension by mutual process
Into means, and thence the directory of endless

*

Aquamaniles used to come in colorful guises
People and monsters joined in practical devices

*

Is circuitous like memory in a snake.
You follow the coastline for several miles, then forsake

*

A large patch of dandelions, the sense that light
Has curled back into the eye — a *figment* of sight

*

A theory may be true and also a puzzle
As good weather includes an occasional light drizzle

*

Cartwheeled bolted to the explosion that worked
By individual decoy which for once unfrocked

*

The way "blue sky" is an appropriate term
Emitting a clear redundancy, like a germ

*

As beautiful as a jar that holds the Beautiful
For centuries — or until the *idea* is full

*

All landscape and consequently all distance
Are wings, to which the essential substance

*

Raspberries being the perverse lachrymae
Confusing time and space. As for civic decay

Poem

Who prop, thou ask'st, in these bad days, my mind
and who, without a single exception, would get up
and fall over into a plate of spaghetti, floating in a vast
vat of green tea.
And why so much thought? One would like to
think, and be thought, yet the sky strewn with marigolds
thickens under its second coat, from the widest
angle in which persons round corners
without so much as a hint that they are paint,
and while each coat counts, in this semi-official and
      chromatic life.

People And Buildings

The answer is to be one with daylight,
which doesn't support the question. The light bends,
people and buildings are swept into the night

like shaved notions of ideas, bright
knowledgeable and containing countless addenda.
The answer is to be one with daylight.

Not that painting scalds everything to a white
brilliance in which to see means as true ends —
people and buildings are swept into the night

along with other versions of their tightly
organized consciousnesses, nerve ends.
The answer is to be one with daylight

which approaches along a slate of brightening
occurrence in which means and would-be ends
like people and buildings are swept into the night

to recur with meaning and occasional delight
of a piece with dawn and its staggered ends.
The answer is to be one with daylight
but people and buildings are swept into the night.

Lineups II

September ss
April 2b
October lf
June cf
December 1b
March 3b
January rf
July c
May p

Frog 3b
Lightning Bug 2b
Cat lf
Dog cf
Hamster 1b
Turtle c
Rabbit ss
Alligator rf
Parakeet p

Wittgenstein lf
Heidegger 2b
Aristotle 1b
Kant rf
Hegel cf
Hume ss
Sartre 3b
Plotinus c
Plato p

Javelin 2b
110 m. high hurdles ss
100 m. dash lf
1500 m. run cf
Long jump rf
400 m. dash 3b
Pole vault 1b
Shotput c
4 x 400 m. relay p

(for Mary Ferrari)

"Composed Upon Westminster Bridge" ss
"The Lucy Poems" 2b
Preface to Lyrical Ballads lf
"Tintern Abbey" cf
"Resolution and Independence" rf
"Michael" 1b
"Mutability" 3b
"The Leech Gatherer" c
"Ode: Intimations of Immortality" p

63

Clover cf
Chicory 3b
Daisy ss
Sunflower lf
Thistle 1b
Dandelion rf
Queen Anne's Lace 2b
Milkweed c
Honeysuckle p

Simenon lf
Sjöwall (Wahlöö) ss
Conan Doyle cf
Chandler 1b
Leonard rf
Chesterton 2b
Christie 3b
Hammett c
Poe p

Pun ss
Paradox lf
Metaphor cf
Simile rf
Hyperbole 1b
Metonymy 3b
Irony c
Understatement 2b
Zeugma p

Mint 3b
Rosemary ss
Thyme lf
Salt 1b
Garlic c
Oregano rf
Dry Mustard cf
Vanilla 2b
Nutmeg p

Williams ss
Hornsby cf
DiMaggio 1b
Ruth c
Mays 3b
Boggs rf
Aaron 2b
Sisler lf
Cobb p

DH Series II

MONTHS — November
PETS — Gecko
PHILOSOPHERS — Derrida
TRACK & FIELD — Marathon
WORDSWORTH — *The Prelude*
WILDFLOWERS — Goldenrod
MYSTERY WRITERS — Spillane
FIGURES OF SPEECH — Synecdoche
HERBS & SPICES — Peppercorn
HITTERS — Mattingly

ALL-STARS Series II

1b Hamster
2b Chesterton
 ss Pun
3b March
 lf Wittgenstein
 cf Clover
 rf Kant/Oregano
  c "The Leech Gatherer"
  p Cobb
dh November

Baseball As A Fact Of Life

A simulated pie crust of poured concrete, with pitchfork marks slicing through every so often to let sun and people in and out. Strips and bellies, pets and projects, peanut shells, vocalise — no! At the far end someone crouched, apparently examining something. As I watch he raises a hand to his cheek, rakes downward in a distinctly *unheimlich* maneuver; appears to unroll a strip of Scotch tape from under the rim of his fedora — in fact he's dressed rather nattily, somewhat in the manner of a 30's saxophone player — first around his hairline, then down around one side of his forehead, along the cheekbone and underneath his nose, which he scrunches down, while curling his upper lip up to hold the tape in place (giving that portion between upper lip and nostrils the air of a mostly transparent moustache which the wearer would, when all was said and done, be just as happy to have off; also an odd expression, something like that of a professional balloon blower), next feeding it into his mouth where he does something obscure with his tongue, out the other side and around his chin

all the while continuing his *lecture* — for that is what I am now aware his posture has signified from the start — on the faults, numbering in the legions, of my baseball lineups. I realize that what I have been taking all the while as concentration has been his utter and consummate displeasure at the quality, organization, publication, copyrighting, and sheer space-displacement of a series of list poems I wrote some twelve years earlier, inspired (I hoped) by the nonpareil French poet Arthur Rimbaud. In an instant it is as though

71

there is no "as though" about it: my entire life has been occupied by this dark room, I have no idea whether night follows day, whether the sun has ever in fact shone on the earth, or whether I have returned from my monthly trip to Lyons or am just starting out as tour guide on a new one.

* * *

This critic for *Cahiers du Cinéma*, whom I will call Arthur, is wonderful at devastating my movie lineup. For some odd reason *The Baker's Wife* by Marcel Pagnol is the most heinous inclusion, and among the capital sins of omission Italian movies of the 60's, the very thought of them, sends him into paroxysms of rage. I try—*not* to defend my selections, which to me was never the point, those being as often as not the given, the world among other versions of it, so that arranging them in baseball terms deranges the same world; while rearranging it, I dared to hope, in an outrageous but valid way, valid (if at all) the way the teen-age years are valid: *cleat-like*: both, as F. T. Prince might say, leave a skid mark.

"You don't know anything *about* American baseball!" I shout. "You don't even know how to pronounce the word!"

But by this point he no longer seems to notice my presence, much less take in my protestations in his fourth or fifth language, EFL, and the theater has begun to whir and sputter, the prelude to an explosion. I am about to shout something further about his *world-wide* ignorance of both baseball and movies

—I am, for example, the only one in the universe who knows he originally forged his press card, and that although born in France in some obscure *département* known only for its boots and fragrant nights, he speaks only phonetic French, lip-synching, when he can manage that, to a cassette player he wears underneath the back of his shirt collar like the Marx Brothers with their Maurice Chevalier imitations in *Monkey Business*, the collaborator on permanent skids — barely enough, in fact, to make it past the ushers in the moonlight cinémathèque in whatever town he happens to be conceptualizing in, and often finding his seat by the purest of pure chance —

when he turns and from evident light years away fixes me with the most penetrating and blinding stare I have ever encountered.

*   *   *

The street outside is quiet now save for an occasional cough, a tardy dog wandering among loose scraps and peels of conversation. I am holding my breath, in both hands, locked somehow in the swollen moment which is time illuminated, when his cheek

goes pink
then scarlet
while unearthly sounds stir
from some impenetrable
coign in his being
as though the blood

circulating through his major organs
has turned to uncut rubies

"I'll —!"

I am about to say, to my later and infinite humiliation, that I am
willing to *edit*, at least the movie lineup, when I am stopped in my
mental tracks. He is now in profile, hunched over as I first wit-
nessed him, his entire being involved in whatever has produced
his current mental and physical state, which has begun to produce
in me a tinge of sympathy along with the antipathy one naturally
feels towards sheer evil or self-promotion ("Good news! I've just
come out with the definitive book in your field!"), with the same
thin strip of curling tape proceeding mysteriously from his hat,
underneath his nose, and towards the bottom of his facial structure.

An international movie, with titles and credits from five or six
nations, fans out from his one blinding eye I can see, framed by
his head now dark gray and metallic, to the wall opposite, through
a small window, and out into the night across a pitch-black street
to another wall belonging to an unprepossessing building stand-
ing among others of mixed use. Within the triangle thus formed
by eye and radiating light, all dust and glow, a great many people
are standing in line before a doorway, among them Michelangelo
Antonioni, Federico Fellini, Ingmar Bergman, Alfred Hitchcock,
Marcel Carné, Jean Renoir, Alain Tanner, Akira Kurosawa, and
Jerry Lewis, together with the two typical Englishmen from *The
Lady Vanishes*, Ray Bolger in his farmer's overalls, Jean Simmons
wet from the Glory version of *Blue Lagoon*, Randolph and Lizabeth

74

Scott, Eddie Constantine — and the line is moving forward slowly and evenly without diminishing into the low, light gray building. The sun comes out bright and warm overhead.

Pan bagna vendors stroll this way and that on the paved walk lining the beach. Across the boulevard a small dinner party is being given for the *monstres* of modern cinema. The air is a sea of garlic, soupe au pistou, bouillabaisse. Seagulls and car horns. Many of the greatest figures of the auteur era, the pre-auteur era, and post-auteur California ("There's much too much snew in the second reel." "What's *snew?*" "Nothing much. What's new with you?") and, strangest to say, someone who looks exactly like Allen Funt wearing full catcher's gear — although to be perfectly candid, Allen Funt looked a good deal like my father at a particular time in the mid-life of both, a period spanning as much as fifteen years; until both men inextricably involved with their cameras and their spools begin to merge not so much with each other as with the silent rapid free-float of non-poetic images from brightness to the mobile dark, with the additional help of an appreciative audience weaned on *8½* and the cast of the original *Mash*, infinitely and uncritically dark and still — or if in motion obscurely so while the lights continue to flicker, bright and dark as day.